Monticello

The Home of Thomas Jefferson

CHARLOTTESVILLE, VIRGINIA

MONTICELLO stands today, a living monument, to Thomas Jefferson who designed and supervised its construction.

The estate on which Monticello was erected came to Thomas Jefferson from his father, Peter Jefferson, who received it as a grant in 1735. The idea of building a beautiful home on top of the little mountain was first conceived by Thomas Jefferson, when as a boy, he played and studied under the trees there. The plans for Monticello were started in 1767, and the work of leveling the site for the building began the following year. However, construction did not begin for several years, and because of numerous changes and alterations the three story house of thirty-five rooms was not completed until after 1809. The house as it is seen today, is the product of Mr. Jefferson's creative and ingenious mind.

He called his home "Monticello" which in Italian means "Little Mountain". He liked the musical sound of the Italian pronunciation, "Montichello," and so the place is called and pronounced today.

The Monticello plantation site is unique. The artificially created plateau is 857 feet above sea level. To make all parts of the mountain accessible, Jefferson constructed on its slopes at four different levels, paths or roundabouts. There are still evidences of these today.

Most of the material for the building was made on the place. The stones for the foundation were quarried from the mountain side, bricks were burned in his own kiln, the timbers cut from his forest, and the nails wrought in his own nailery. Even some of the hardware for the Mansion was made in his shop, but such things as locks, glass for the doors and windows were purchased.

In those days there was on every plantation a series of small disconnected out-buildings, such as laundry, smoke house, dairy, stables, weaving house and kitchen. With his architectural genius, Jefferson sought to make these as inconspicuous as possible by locating them beneath the long terraces terminating in two balanced out-chambers. Connecting these terraces is the all-weather passageway in which are strategically placed the wine room, beer room, and ware room.

The first building erected was the small pavilion at the end of the south terrace. It was completed in time for Jefferson to bring his bride, Martha Wayles Skelton, a charming widow of 23, there in January 1772. Thus the southwest out-chamber is referred to appropriately as the "Honeymoon Cottage". The marriage was a happy one, though of short duration, for after only ten years Martha passed away. They had six children, five daughters and one son. Only one of whom, Martha, the eldest, survived her father. Another daughter, Mary, grew to womanhood, married, but died when only 26.

In 1769 young Tom Jefferson became a member of the Virginia House of Burgesses, and thus began a remarkable career of unselfish devotion to a nation he helped to found and build. He served as a delegate to the Continental Congress (where he was chosen to draft the Declaration of Independence), Governor of Virginia, Minister to France, Secretary of State under George Washington, Vice-President of the United States, two terms as President (1801-1809), and founder of the University of Virginia.

When Mr. Jefferson returned from France, he made numerous changes in the plan and design of Monticello. An early floor plan contained a central stairway to the second floor, but this was eliminated, and he constructed two very narrow winding staircases, one in each wing.

While abroad he purchased many accessories and ornaments for his beloved Monticello — silver, china, candlesticks, linens and works of art — things not readily obtainable in America.

Many of the original furnishings are on display on the first floor of the Mansion. Some of Mr. Jefferson's innovations, still in use, are the seven day calendar clock with its cannon-ball weights, and the double doors between the Hall and Parlour, which open simultaneously when either is moved. A weather vane on top of the portico is connected to a dial on the ceiling beneath, and can be read from inside the house. Built into the mantle in the Dining Room are two small dumb-waiters, one on each end, which were used to carry bottles of wine from the cellar. All of the beds are located in alcoves, and in Mr. Jefferson's bedroom the alcove also opens into the study.

Following Mr. Jefferson's retirement to Monticello, he had a continuous stream of visitors from far and near. Many stayed for days, weeks and even months. Monticello was by far the most interesting and attractive home in America, and Jefferson's engaging personality made these visits most enjoyable. Naturally, this was a tremendous drain on the resources of Monticello and Jefferson's last years were marred by never ending financial worries.

Thomas Jefferson died at Monticello, July 4, 1826, at the age of 83. He is buried in the family cemetery on the mountain side.

With the passing of Thomas Jefferson, Monticello and its furnishings were sold to liquidate the debts of the estate.

In 1923, almost one hundred years after the death of Thomas Jefferson, the estate was purchased by the THOMAS JEFFERSON MEMORIAL FOUNDATION. Monticello was in ruins. The Mansion had suffered from the neglect of the many occupants. who had neither the funds nor the interest in preserving the buildings. Gradually the Foundation has restored the estate. Through research, repair and restoration the Monticello you see today, is the Monticello of Mr. Jefferson's day.

East Front

Entrance hall showing Seven Day Clock designed by Jefferson.

Entrance hall looking toward
drawing room and showing balcony.

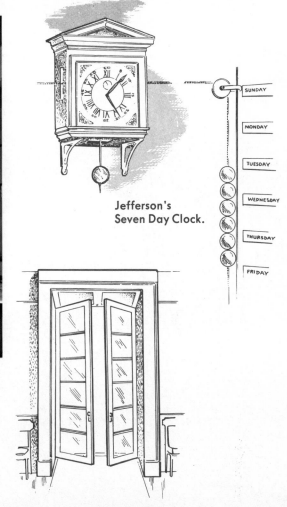

Jefferson's
Seven Day Clock.

SUNDAY

MONDAY

TUESDAY

WEDNESDAY

THURSDAY

FRIDAY

Automatic Glass Doors
to drawing room.

Jefferson's bedroom showing his alcove bed, chaise lounge and work table.

Library

Bedroom of Martha Jefferson Randolph, showing original highboy.

Double windows and curtains designed by Jefferson.

Jefferson's Piano.

Madison Room or
North Octagonal Room.

Monroe Room or
North Square Room.

Parlour

Dining Room

Revolving
serving door.

Tearoom

Coffee Urn designed
by Jefferson.

Mantel with
Wedgwood inserts
and dumb-waiter.

View of Charlottesville and
University of Virginia
as seen from North Terrace.

Kitchen

Quartet Music Stand.

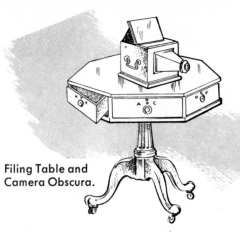

Filing Table and
Camera Obscura.

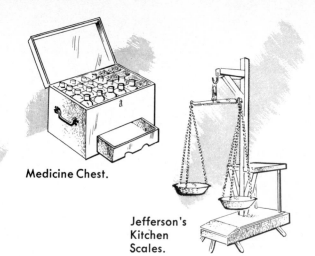

Medicine Chest.

Jefferson's
Kitchen
Scales.

Stairway at
Monticello
with 24" treads.

Passageway
under Monticello.

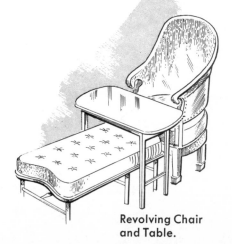

Revolving Chair
and Table.

Honeymoon Lodge, slave quarters and summer kitchen.

Interior of Honeymoon Lodge, at end of south terrace.

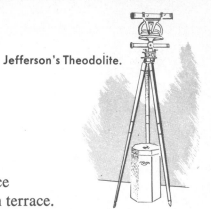

Jefferson's Theodolite.

Law Office
and north terrace.

Jefferson's Gig.

West Front
Reflection Pool.

View of
Piedmont Valley.

Here was buried Thomas Jefferson,
Author of the Declaration of American Independence
of the Statute of Virginia for Religious Freedom
and Father of the University of Virginia.

Born April 13, 1743   Died July 4, 1826

"all my wishes end where
I hope my days will end
...at MONTICELLO"

Rotunda of University of Virginia
and serpentine wall designed by Thomas Jefferson.

Jefferson Memorial
and cherry blossoms.

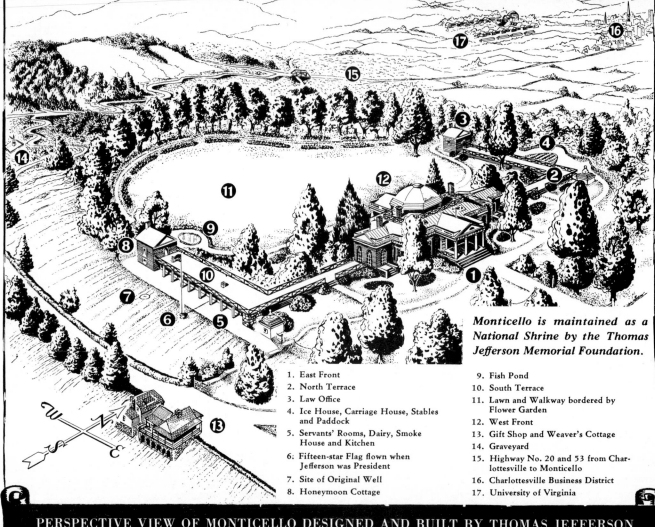

Monticello is maintained as a National Shrine by the Thomas Jefferson Memorial Foundation.

1. East Front
2. North Terrace
3. Law Office
4. Ice House, Carriage House, Stables and Paddock
5. Servants' Rooms, Dairy, Smoke House and Kitchen
6. Fifteen-star Flag flown when Jefferson was President
7. Site of Original Well
8. Honeymoon Cottage
9. Fish Pond
10. South Terrace
11. Lawn and Walkway bordered by Flower Garden
12. West Front
13. Gift Shop and Weaver's Cottage
14. Graveyard
15. Highway No. 20 and 53 from Charlottesville to Monticello
16. Charlottesville Business District
17. University of Virginia

PERSPECTIVE VIEW OF MONTICELLO DESIGNED AND BUILT BY THOMAS JEFFERSON